**EPIC BOOKS** are no ordinary books. They burst with intense action, high-speed heroics, and shadows of the unknown. Are you ready for an Epic adventure?

This edition first published in 2023 by Bellwether Media, Inc.

No part of this publication may be reproduced in whole or in part without written permission of the publisher. For information regarding permission, write to Bellwether Media, Inc., Attention: Permissions Department, 6012 Blue Circle Drive, Minnetonka, MN 55343.

Library of Congress Cataloging-in-Publication Data

LC record for Lamborghini Huracán Evo available at: https://lccn.loc.gov/2022020242

Text copyright © 2023 by Bellwether Media, Inc. EPIC and associated logos are trademarks and/or registered trademarks of Bellwether Media, Inc.

Editor: Kieran Downs    Designer: Jeffrey Kollock

Printed in the United States of America, North Mankato, MN

# TABLE OF CONTENTS

| A FAST LAUNCH | 4 |
| ALL ABOUT THE HURACÁN EVO | 6 |
| PARTS OF THE HURACÁN EVO | 12 |
| THE HURACÁN'S FUTURE | 20 |
| GLOSSARY | 22 |
| TO LEARN MORE | 23 |
| INDEX | 24 |

# A FAST LAUNCH

The driver stomps the gas pedal. The engine roars as the car launches forward. The ride is smooth.

The driver steers the car around a corner. The car darts out of sight. The Lamborghini Huracán Evo is crazy fast!

# ALL ABOUT THE HURACÁN EVO

1965 350GTV

Lamborghini started making cars in 1963. The company's first car was the 350GTV.

Today, workers build Lamborghinis by hand in Sant'Agata Bolognese, Italy. They only use machines to move heavy parts around. Popular Lamborghinis include the Murciélago, Urus, and Aventador.

URUS

## WHERE IS IT MADE?

EUROPE

SANT'AGATA BOLOGNESE, ITALY

Lamborghini introduced the Huracán in 2013. It replaced the popular Gallardo. The Huracán Performante came out in 2017.

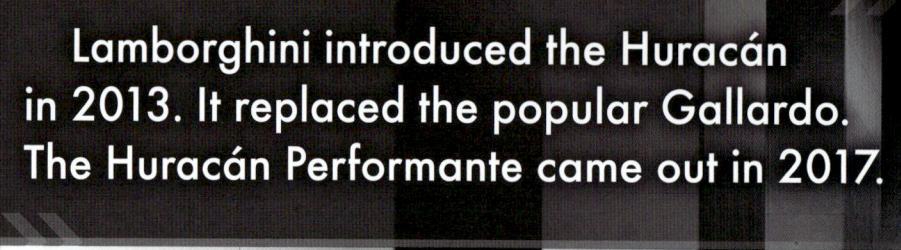
GALLARDO

HURACÁN PERFORMANTE

### STRONG AS A BULL

The Huracán is named after a Spanish fighting bull from the late 1800s. *Huracán* means "hurricane" in Spanish.

The Evo is the newest car in the Huracán line. It came out in 2019. It uses the Performante's **V10 engine**.

The Huracán Evo's body is made for style and speed. Its shape is based on a shark. It looks sleek. Even the headlights and taillights have sharp looks.

# HURACÁN EVO BASICS

**YEAR FIRST MADE** 2019

**COST** starts at $213,104

**HOW MANY MADE** unknown

HEADLIGHT

## FEATURES

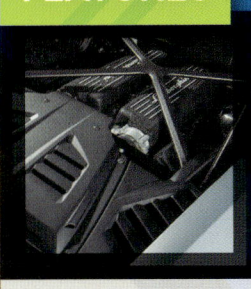
V10 engine

all-wheel steering

rear spoiler

# PARTS OF THE HURACÁN EVO

The Evo has a V10 engine. Unlike other **supercars**, it does not have **turbochargers**. Its engine does not **compress** the air it pulls in. Instead, the air provides power right away. This gives the engine its loud roar!

## ENGINE SPECS

**V10 ENGINE**

**TOP SPEED** | 202 miles (325 kilometers) per hour

**0-60 TIME** | 2.6 seconds

**HORSEPOWER** | 631 hp

The Evo has good **aerodynamics**. The front bumper has openings to let air in. This air movement keeps the car on the road.

The rear **spoiler** creates **downforce**. This gives the car better control.

### WITH FLIGHT IN MIND

The shape of the Evo's rear spoiler is based on the rear part of a bird's back.

SPOILER

The Evo features all-wheel steering. This helps the car stay **stable** at high speeds.

**WELL-CENTERED CAR**

The Evo's engine sits in the center of the car. This helps the car go fast around corners.

Steering, braking, and shifting are controlled by a computer. The computer can adjust the **traction** control for each wheel.

A **touch screen** controls the radio and temperature inside the Evo. It also has voice control!

TOUCH SCREEN

## SIZE CHART

**WIDTH** 76.1 inches (193.3 centimeters)

Switches control things like the hood and power windows. These switches look like they were taken from a fighter jet!

SWITCHES

HEIGHT 45.9 inches (116.5 centimeters)

LENGTH 178 inches (452 centimeters)

# THE HURACÁN'S FUTURE »

Lamborghini will make more Huracáns. The Evo's **convertible** is called the Spyder. The Huracán STO is a race car approved for road driving.

Lamborghini next plans to make a **hybrid** Huracán. The Huracán's future looks exciting!

HURACÁN SPYDER

### FOLLOW ME

Some airports use "follow me" cars. They guide airplanes on the ground. In Bologna, Italy, a Huracán Evo sometimes does the job.

**HURACÁN STO**

# GLOSSARY

**aerodynamics**—the system on a sports car that is designed to help it move easily and quickly

**compress**—to squeeze to fit into a smaller space

**convertible**—a car with a folding or soft roof

**downforce**—a force that pushes a car down to the road

**hybrid**—using both a gasoline engine and an electric motor for power

**spoiler**—a part on the back of the car that helps the car grip the road

**stable**—not likely to lose control

**supercars**—expensive and high-performing sports cars

**touch screen**—a display on which people can select options by touching the screen

**traction**—a force that keeps something from slipping on a surface

**turbochargers**—engine parts that force high-pressure air into the engine to create extra power

**V10 engine**—an engine with 10 cylinders arranged in the shape of a "V"

# TO LEARN MORE

## AT THE LIBRARY

Adamson, Thomas K. *Lamborghini Sián*. Minneapolis, Minn.: Bellwether Media, 2023.

Doeden, Matt. *Sports Cars*. North Mankato, Minn.: Capstone Press, 2019.

Storm, Marysa. *Supercars*. Mankato, Minn.: Black Rabbit Books, 2020.

## ON THE WEB

**FACTSURFER**

Factsurfer.com gives you a safe, fun way to find more information.

1. Go to www.factsurfer.com.

2. Enter "Lamborghini Huracán Evo" into the search box and click 🔍.

3. Select your book cover to see a list of related content.

# INDEX

aerodynamics, 14
air, 12, 14
airports, 21
all-wheel steering, 16, 17
basics, 11
body, 10
braking, 17
bumper, 14
company, 6, 8, 20
computer, 17
convertible, 20
downforce, 15
engine, 4, 9, 12, 16
engine specs, 12
headlights, 10, 11
history, 6, 8, 9
hybrid, 20
models, 6, 7, 8, 9, 20
name, 9

Sant'Agata Bolognese, Italy, 7
shifting, 17
size chart, 18–19
speed, 5, 10, 16
spoiler, 15
Spyder, 20
STO, 20, 21
supercars, 12
switches, 19
taillights, 10
touch screen, 18
traction control, 17
voice control, 18

The images in this book are reproduced through the courtesy of: Lamborghini, front cover, pp. 1, 3, 4, 4-5, 6-7, 8 (Gallardo), 8-9 (left), 8-9 (right), 10-11, 11 (isolated, engine, steering, spoiler), 12, 12-13, 14-15, 15 ,16, 16-17, 17, 18, 18 (width), 18-19 (length), 19, 20-21 (left), 20-21 (right); Sergey Kohl, p. 6.